Lawrence Qu

G000108222

Rise of the Slaves

Table of Content

- The origin of the Slavs
- The name "Slavs" in other written sources.
- Searching for the Slavs' "homeland"
- Modern views
-

  "Long history" of the Slavs
- The problem of Indo-European languages
- First europe
- Original headquarters
- "Old European" stage
- Breakup of Old European people. Establishment of Baltoslavs and Praslavs
- Opinions of archaeologists on the ethnogenesis of Slavs
- Autochthonists and Allochtonists
- Cultural continuity?
- Relations of ancient authors
- Lugii
- Weneds
- Ptolemy's "Sarmation"
- Weds - "Praslavs"?
- A new approach to the ethnogenesis of the Slavs

The origin of the Slavs

The name "Slavs" appears in sources only in the sixth century. The first, direct, and related to the Slavs in written sources also come from the same period. The first of which I would like to mention is the testimony of a Gothic historian, probably of Germanic origin - Jordanes. In the middle of the sixth century, he wrote in his work Getik, or About the origin and history of the Goths:

Inside them (here are the Tisza, Danube and unidentified Flutausis rivers) is Dacia, crowned with steep Alps (Carpathians), and along their left slope, which tends to the west, settled starting from the sources of Winkel, in immeasurable areas the Wened people. Wenedów, although their variable names are now, applied to various strains, they are mainly called their Sklavens and Antes.

In the next fragment of the work Jordanes tried to define more precisely the seats of the Sklawens and Antes:

The Sklawens live from the city of Nowietunum and the lake called Mursiański to Danastru (Dniester), and north to Winkli; those in the place of cities have mud and forests. And the Anas, who are the bravest of them, stretch to Danastr, where Pontus (Black Sea) bends, to Danapru (Dnieper), which rivers are many days away from each other.

I will return to the work of Jordanes later in this chapter. Getik is, therefore, the first written source in which the name "Slavs" (Sklavens) can be found.

The name "Slavs" in other written sources.

In Latin sources, starting from Jordanes, you can still find various forms of the current name: Sclavini, Sclaveni, Sclavi. Also Greek sources give the names: Sklabeoni, Sthlabeoi, and in Slavic, you can also find other characters: Slovene, Slovane, Slavs. Despite the fact that the name sounds as if it were of native origin, its source is not entirely clear. The thesis that historians consider the most likely is that the word Slavs means "their people." Other meanings attributed are: "inhabitants of the area near the river or lake called Slova, Slava," or from the nickname - "slow man, growler". Researchers also claimed that the name Slavs accompanied from the first moment the appearance of Slavic peoples in historical sources. It occurs in a dual sense: it covers both the whole of the Slavic peoples and some of the Slavic peoples, and what is specific - they were peoples living on the periphery of the

Slavic world, in the vicinity of non-Slavic peoples (South Slavic Slovenes, Novgorod Slovenes, Slavs in Pomerania).

Searching for the Slavs' "homeland"

Two questions remain: where were the original Slavs' headquarters and what happened with the Slavs in the period preceding the sixth century.

Already in the Middle Ages there were attempts to answer this question. Unknown, probably living at the turn of the seventh and eighth centuries, the author of the cosmographic treaty - called the cosmographer or Geographer of Ravenna - believed that the Slavs came from Scythia, which, however, tells us little because of the inability of modern historians to determine the geographical location of this concept in the early Middle Ages . The later author (ninth century) called the Bavarian geographer, writing about Zeriuani - one of the Slavic tribes said that all their Slavic tribes originate from their country and, as they say, they originate. It cannot be said with certainty what is hidden under the name Zeriuani. She appears twice at the Bavarian Bavarian Geographer. Regardless of whether Zeriuani in the work of the Bavarian Geographer is Siewierz (Ruthenian, in the Desna basin or in Bulgaria) or Serbs (rather Balkan, since the Elbe source is mentioned elsewhere) or other tribes - maybe not we will find out who and for what purpose he gave the East French author such information and whether the Slavs in the ninth century did indeed believe that all of them came from the territory of Zeriuani.

In the eleventh or early twelfth century in the territory of the holy Russian state, i.e. the area of eastern Slavic land near Kiev, which occupied the first place in terms of social and cultural development, a writing profession was created, i.e. simply a chronicle of the pen of an unknown author, traditionally called Nestor. In this novel of past years (Povest 'vremennych let) one can find the first extensive, and at the same Slavic origin, genealogical argument of the Slavs.

The starting point for the genealogy of the Slavic peoples for Nestor was the Holy Bible. Following the tradition widely accepted in Christian literature, the author referred to the three sons of Patriarch Noah, from whom all seventy-two peoples of the world were to be descended. Descendants of Noah's eldest son, Shem, were to rule in the East, the youngest, Ham - in the south, and the sons of Japhet were to receive countries in the west and north. This biblical separation of nations and languages was to take place with the destruction of the Tower of Babel, later Nestor explained the origin of various Slavic tribes. At this point, the question about the path of the ancestors of the Slavs from the south, from the Middle East, which according to historians was to be the matrix of all peoples to the north, is imposed.

And from these seventy-two nations there was a Slavic nation, Nestor wrote, from the Jafet tribe - Noreks, who are Slavs. And from these seventy-two nations there was a Slavic nation, Nestor wrote, from the Jafet tribe - Noreks, who are Slavs.

In medieval Poland, as in the Czech Republic at the time, interest in Slavicism as a whole was low. It was not until the fourteenth century that a man unknown by name was supplemented by interpolation of a similarly unknown by Kronika Wielkopolski, whose framework was probably created at the end of the 13th century. In this way he tried to link the history of Poland with the history of Slavs. He did it with an idea, but subjectively. Let's listen to the interpolator's story:

In the oldest chronicles they write that Panonia is the mother and cradle of all Slavic nations. The same assumption as at Nestor's, although the anonymous interpolator from the Greater Poland Chronicle certainly did not read the Russian pen. What led him to this belief, apart from the "oldest books", which, unfortunately, cannot be defined more precisely. "Greek," according to the Greek and Slavic translation, is called someone possessing everything, and according to that in Slavic, "the gentleman" is called a magnum (...). At this point, an unknown Wielkopolan gives two linguistic and biblical arguments. Well, they say that these Pannonian people, named after the Lord, are derived, as they say, from Janus, a descendant of Jafet (...) From these Pananians came three brothers, sons of the Lord, rulers of the Pannans, whose original name was Lech, the other Rus, third Czech. And these three offspring, of themselves and their family, had three kingdoms: Lechites, rubies and Czechs (they were also called Bobemi), they have them now and in the future they will have as long as God's will pleases them.

In the further part of the interpolation regarding the origin of the Slavs, the unknown author listed and described various Slavic peoples and tribes, especially from the area of southern Slavic and Połabia, not to mention the Ruthenians, supplementing his arguments according to the etymologies of the tribal names at the time.

Modern views

In the further part of the interpolation regarding the origin of the Slavs, the unknown author listed and described various Slavic peoples and tribes, especially from the area of southern Slavic and Połabia, not to mention the Ruthenians, supplementing his arguments according to the etymologies of the tribal names at the time. Modern views I am not going to continue here this interesting argument in what way the Slavs themselves imagined their own origin in the more distant past. Opinion that Panonia was the cradle of Slavic peoples did not stand the test of time due to insufficient evidence. I do not want to present here "pre-scientific" attempts to solve the problem, e.g. by identifying specific Slavs with ancient Lyre, Sarmatians or Germanic Vandals. At this point I would like to go to the merits of my research problem.

At some point, modern science ceased to be satisfied with the simple prescriptions of chroniclers from the last two centuries. Many efforts have been made to identify the issue in question. A closer look at hundreds of scientific papers on the ethnogenesis of Slavs, containing dozens of hypotheses and theories, can set not only historians pessimistic about the cognitive possibilities of science. The generally accepted theory of Slavic ethnogenesis has not been created and will not be created soon enough. Meanwhile, I think that there has been progress in research into the ethnogenesis of Slavs, because nowadays one can safely put forward various scientifically correct theories on this topic. Perhaps at some point the views of historians, ethnologists and archaeologists on this issue will come closer.

"Long history" of the Slavs

Traditional views with all their diversity, and even mutual exclusion, the vast majority of theories about the origin of the Slavs so far formulated had one common assumption that the origins of the Slavs were dated well before the 6th century, when their name appeared in written sources. This thesis implies that the Slavs already had long centuries of their own Slav history in the sixth century.

The question arises that since the Slavs existed before the sixth century, why the ancient authors did not write anything about them in their writings. In general, there is no mention of Slavs in the source material, both written and epigraphic from antiquity. According to some researchers of the history of Slavs, the answer is simple. The ancient world was simply not interested in the part of the land that was then inhabited by the Slavs. But isn't this answer a simplification of the matter? It really depends on where the alleged headquarters of the Slavs of the last centuries of antiquity were located, and this certainly cannot be said. If, as many scholars want - including probably most Polish prehistorists - in Central Europe, north of the Sudetes and the Carpathians, the silence of the ancient authors about the Slavs is quite incomprehensible.

Methodological assumptions would require that if there are no arguments contradicting this thesis, in the last at least in the period before the sixth century, the Priests occupied identical seats or at least similar to those of the Slavs in the sixth and seventh centuries. It should then be assumed that from this area the Slavs came and headed during their great expansion at the beginning of the Middle Ages to the territories of the Czech Basin, Slovakia, Pannonia, the Balkan Peninsula, and the Połabszczyzna region. Areas mentioned in the previous sentence should be supplemented with areas occupied by the Slavs in the north-east, at the expense of the Balts, and in the south-east, at the expense of the Iranian peoples, and would these be the original seats of the Slavs, and maybe even their "primeval"?

From this point on, I would like to avoid the term "fatherland" if it is possible. This term is burdened with the stigma of static account of history, which says that a certain people has always existed and developed in a certain area. Meanwhile, in history, the word always makes no sense either. One can only write and speak about a longer or shorter stay of a people on a given territory. Fatherland, in the strict sense of the word, would only be such an area in which the formation of a given people took place. Meanwhile, this assumption is erroneous, because it is extremely difficult to determine the moment when most European peoples have formed, mainly because of the long distance in time.

If several extreme theories are rejected, which are hardly found in modern science (e.g. the Danube, Lesser-Asian or Asian theories), views on the original headquarters of the Praslavs can be generally divided into Eastern and Western. Due to the meridional direction of the great rivers of the European Lowlands and the stability of this natural element, individual theories have become accustomed to the names of rivers within which the "Slavic" homeland would be located. Here are the most important of the theory along with the names of their supporters:

the Połabsko-Wiślańska theory (Józef Kostrzewski,
Konrad Jaźdżewski),
Odrzańsko-Bużański theory (Tadeusz Lepr-Spławiński),
Elbe-Dnieper theory (P. N. Tretiakow),
Odra-Dnieper theory (Witold Hensel),

The Vistula-Dnieper theory (Karol Muullenhofft,
Lubor Niederle),
the Dnieper theory (Jan Rozwadowski, J. Rostafiński).

The aforementioned list of theories does not exhaust the diversity of views expressed in science. Often, the scholars themselves sometimes changed their views on the issue we raised. I would like to return to some names from the list and theory. At this point, I would like to familiarize the reader with the source foundations of this diversity of views, and also reach the very source of the controversy.

Representatives of various sciences have put in work trying to explain the ethnogenesis of Slavs. At this point I would like to take a look at the basic findings of linguists and archaeologists, and then answer the question of how helpful ancient written sources can be.

The aforementioned list of theories does not exhaust the diversity of views expressed in science. Often, the scholars themselves sometimes changed their views on the issue we raised. I would like to return to some names from the list and theory. At this point, I would like to familiarize the reader with the source foundations of this diversity of views, and also reach the very source of the controversy.

Representatives of various sciences have put in work trying to explain the ethnogenesis of Slavs. At this point I would like to take a look at the basic findings of linguists and archaeologists, and then answer the question of how helpful ancient written sources can be.

The problem of Indo-European languages

I will not go back to the history of linguistics before the nineteenth century, when researchers noticed that all the languages we use in Europe except languages such as Finnish, Hungarian and Pyrenean Basques, languages from various places on earth where the expansion of Europeans arrived, as well as some languages extinct, which were spoken in the past: Latin, ancient Persians and Hindus exhibit many common characteristics. Linguists divide European languages into three large groups: Romance, e.g. French, Spanish, Romanian, Italian; Germanic e.g. German, English, Norwegian and Slavic e.g. Polish, Russian, Czech, Belarusian, Serbo-Croatian. In addition to these three groups, there are also so-called "residual" languages, such as Celtic, e.g. Irish, Gaelic and Lyric, e.g. Albanian. Once, these languages were spoken in much of Europe. Between Slavic languages, just like between Germanic and Romance languages. It is much harder to find similarities between, for example, Polish and German or Italian. The layman will not notice the kinship between these languages, but an experienced linguist will observe them.

Without a doubt, all of these languages are related, although to varying degrees. The same applies to these extinct languages. Due to the fact that historians have confirmed the extent of these related languages, ranging from Europe in the west to India in the east - they were called a group or family of Indo-European languages. This is not the only language family. Next to it existed in the past and currently there are other language groups. Mention may be made of e.g. Altaic, Semitic, Finno-Ugric, Asian. It was often the case that in the past and nowadays peoples speaking these languages were adjacent to peoples called from the language they spoke - "Indo-European".

The similarities between the various Indo-European languages are not uniform and cannot be a matter of chance. They concern word formation and grammar. Added to this is another important observation: over the centuries, in the development of individual Indo-European languages, differences mutually increase, and similarities decrease, e.g. what is interesting, in the Middle Ages Polish was much closer to Czech than it is today. Analogous observations from different periods of time and different regions of the Indo-European language area incline to the bold, but scientifically acceptable and justified hypothesis that the older the period is taken into account in this matter, the smaller the differences between individual Indo-European languages can be found. Probably in a very distant past, there was only one undifferentiated language from which successive Indo-European languages gradually emerged. These languages have varied over the centuries, but the trunk of each of them - the starting point was common.

First europe

The primary language of all later Indo-European languages was called, for lack of a better idea, an Indo-European language. Its existence is hypothetical because its existence cannot be confirmed on the basis of any linguistic monument. Despite the fact that the language was not directly attested, it is now well known to scholars. Scientists came to him during research on various Indo-European languages. Scholars have traced their interrelationships and using language principles proven in other fields, as well as a considerable amount of research ingenuity, have reconstructed a large part of the Proto-Indo-European language. Currently, there are even special dictionaries of this language of considerable volume.

That's all linguists have to say about Pre-Indo-European language. At this point, historians put forward the thesis that, since there was once a pre-Indo-European language, there must also have been a people speaking that language. They were pre-Indo-European people, colloquially Praindo-Europeans. The eminent scholar A. Meillet wrote: the Indo-European people certainly existed, although it is not known exactly where and when. I would like to remind you that its existence is known only from linguistic inquiries, no other written or archaeological sources confirm this. It must have existed a long time ago, because around 2000 B.C. it belonged to history. At the turn of the third and second millennium BC, the Indo-European Hittite people appeared in Asia Minor, moreover, confirmed in sources of the Middle East, which proves the already advanced process of separating separate peoples from Praindo Europeans. One of the most characteristic features of Indo-European peoples was, probably still from the period of the pre-Indo-European community, knowledge of a horse with a harness, and paleozoological studies indicate that the process of domestication of the horse took place in the period between 3000 and 2600 BC. So the community in question here still had to exist. Is it harder to answer the question when it was created? To date, no reliable answer can be given. Maybe it was ahead of the younger Stone Age, which in Central Europe began around 5000 BC, i.e. that it reached Middle Stone Age, or Mesolithic.

To understand many ethnogenesis processes, among others origin of the Slavs, it would be of great importance to determine the original locations where the Preno-Europeans lived before the collapse of this first community. Unfortunately, views and opinions are a bone of contention among researchers. Tadeusz Milewski, an outstanding Polish linguist, characterized the "homeland" of Indo-Europeans as follows:

(...) a country located far from the sea and high mountains, a country with a moderate climate, in which there were no elephants and lions, but wolves and horses, beeches and birches, capable of surviving the period of recurring snow-covered winter.

Original headquarters

This image was created only on the basis of an analysis of the reconstructed language of Praindo-Europeans. The language is vivid and eloquent, but only to a limited extent allows localization of the Prao-Europeans' homeland. It was neither on the sea nor near high mountains. It certainly lay far from the tropics, i.e. in the temperate zone. There is nothing more to say about this. Two concepts clash in science since the last century. The first of them locates the Indo-Europeans' homeland, generally speaking, in the forest zone, because in Eastern Europe the zone was inhabited by Finno-Ugric and Baltic peoples, whose peoples were characterized by permanent residence. So, in practice, forest theory boils down to locating the forefathers of all Indo-Europeans in Europe. The forest theory, i.e. the European one, is opposed to the steppe theory, locating this primeval homeland in the Eurasian steppe, i.e. the Black Sea, Caspian, and Kazakh steppes. Proponents of both theories can cite a number of arguments to support their theses. I will limit myself to expressing my own view and will spare the reader tedious calculating theses and statements. At the current stage of research, steppe theory seems more likely to me.

This theory says that the ancestors of the Slavs, like other European peoples, came to Europe from the east, from the great Eurasian steppe. After all, it took many centuries before Slavs evolved from Praindo Europeans, and this process was, according to archaeological research, much more complicated than previously thought. Nor should it be understood that the Slavs came to their historical headquarters from Asia, although such views appeared in science, although at present rather rarely. The ancestors of the Slavs gradually came from Asia, not the Slavs themselves, who in those distant times did not exist at all.

"Old European" stage

Studies carried out after World War II have shown that in the water nomenclature of significant parts of Europe, except the south: the Pyrenean, partly Apennine, Balkan and northern peninsulas, which is the domain of Finno-Ugric peoples, one can distinguish an ancient layer of names, which is very uniform and characteristic. The water names, especially the river names, have this important feature for the language historian that they generally show amazing durability: the peoples living on the rivers change and leave, but the names created once remain, at most, only slightly changing their form. This feature, for example, does not have the names of human settlements or countries, which usually change according to changes in ethnic relations. The layer of names in question comes from the time before the emergence of later language groups of "European" Indo-Europeans (Celtic,

Illyrian, Germanic, Slavic, etc.), but right after the collapse of the Pro-Indo-European community. Names of this type do not appear in other areas of the Indo-European world, e.g. in Indo-Iranians or Greeks. It follows that, thanks to knowledge of the history and principles of linguistics, one can capture the first phase of Indo-European expansion into Europe. The creators of this expansion were called Old European in science, and their language - Old European.

Breakup of Old European people. Establishment of Baltoslavs and Praslavs

When the Old European community collapsed, and new waves of migration of Indo-European peoples, whose details of the process are still little known and disputed, began to emerge successively, partially existing until today language groups. Pretty quickly, of course, in categories suitable for this type of process, i.e. in centuries, the Tochar broke off, wandering far east to the Chinese border, where they died out in the early Middle Ages. The western and southern branches of "European" Indo-Europeans included Illyrians, Italics and Celts. The northern branch, the most interesting to us here, consisted of the ancestors of the later Germans, Balts and Slavs. Detailed research has shown that in Slavic languages there are as many as 164 words derived from this Germanic-Balto-Slavic community. This is a relatively high number. Then Pragerman broke away and in this way a Balto-Slavic community emerged, documented by the number of 289 Balto-Slavic nouns in Slavic languages. This community existed until about 1000 BC. year and from that moment you can talk about the Praslavs. Another fifth in turn, after the pre-European, Old European, German-Balto-Slavic and Balto-Slavic language community, Praslav, existed for about two millennia, and probably ceased to exist at the beginning of the Middle Ages. According to linguists, until the X-XII century, all Slavs spoke basically one more language, differing only in secondary features of the dialectal type.

Here is how much a linguist can say about the ethnogenesis of the Indo-European peoples of the Slavs. Linguists are already convinced that the area of Slavs' existence should be narrowed to the borders of our continent, but the vast majority of scholars argue in what place of Europe last at least the links of this centuries-old process. The question then arises where finally the ethnogenesis of the Slavs took place? However, this question remains unanswered because comparative linguistics cannot provide a definite solution. Perhaps archaeologists will be able to answer them.

Opinions of archaeologists on the ethnogenesis of Slavs

Around the middle of the fifth millennium BC. peoples living in the Polish lands began, first slowly from the south, then increasingly faster, succumbing to multilateral external influences, to move to a higher "productive" stage of social development. This is how the Neolithic, i.e. the Younger Stone Age, began in Poland. Until now, archaeologists, based on information most often from excavations or accidental finds, are unable to capture the ethnic affiliation of the producers of these finds. They get to know the old peoples only on the basis of their material products preserved to our times, which is associated with using the concept of "archaeological culture". Archaeological culture is the totality of material remnants of its creators available to learn about, clearly distinguishing itself from analogous neighboring monument sets. This concept is useful in archaeological research, but the relationship of individual cultures to the peoples who once created them is not as direct as it once was thought. Archaeological culture could suit one people, the so-called ethos, but it could also include territory inhabited by more than one people. Finally, it could be that the same people were represented by two or more archaeological cultures. However, it does not seem right to be on the side of researchers who negate any possibility of ethnic interpretation of archaeological sources, since historians often use the results of archaeological research in their findings. It is possible to control the results of archaeologists' research by comparing them with the linguists' findings, and also by linguists' considerations - as we approach the turn of the old and new era with testimonies of ancient written sources, although with some limitations.

Autochthonists and Allochtonists

In science until recently, and even today, two views clash: indigenous and allochtonistic. According to the first, the Slavs were "eternal" inhabitants of the lands north of the arch of the Carpathians and the Sudetes. The second says that they came to this land only at the beginning of the V and VI century, that is, in the early Middle Ages. Both of the above-mentioned directions have occurred and occur in many varieties. This is not the place to explain the differences in views in detail. However, one should mention the historical dispute which was important in Polish science and Polish awareness in the interwar years, and continued after World War II between representatives of the so-called Poznań neoautochthonous school and its opponents.

History est magistra vitae is a well-known saying: history is a teacher of life. It fulfills this function differently ... But the reverse of this Latin sentence is also true: Vita est magistra historiae, meaning life is a teacher of history. We have no real influence on this, that we look at the past, whether we intend it or not, through the prism of our experiences from the present. It is important not to bend science at any cost to non-scientific e.g. political goals.

And this has happened more than once in history. German science, undoubtedly leading in the nineteenth and early twentieth centuries in the field of prehistoric research, sometimes pursued more or less consciously the interests of Prussian and German raison d'etat, regarding the origin of the Slavs strongly holding allochtonistic theories. According to this theory, the lands north of the Sudeten and Carpathian Mountains were to be the "eternal" seats of the Germanic tribes: Vandals, Burgundy, Goths, etc. It was only in the fifth and sixth centuries when the Germanic peoples partly moved towards the borders of the Roman Empire, along with the hordes of the wild The slightly less savage Slavic peoples were to invade Hunów on the Vistula and Oder, displacing and destroying what was left of East Germans. It is not surprising that the culture of the lands of later Poland, clear in archaeological material after at least a break since the sixth century, is incomparably more primitive and barbaric than the culture of Germanic tribes of the first centuries of our era, i.e. Roman period). From this point of view, the history of the later expansion of German rulers and feudal lords to the east, first in the Elbe, then to the Czech Republic, Poland, etc., or even modern political and economic expansion, this is about the partitions of Poland and Hakata in the Prussian partition of Germany, lost their aggressive character, because they have become something of a tool of historical justice, regaining those areas which, as belonging to the Germanic world centuries ago, rightly belonged to Germany.

Science was harnessed in this way, exemplified by prehistory, in the service of politics, or more precisely, in the service of Great German imperialism. It is not surprising that science in Slavic countries, mainly in Poland, took a completely different position. Outstanding Polish scholars from Poznań, the archeologist Józef Kostrzewski, anthropologist Jan Czekanowski and historian Kazimierz Tymieniecki, formulated views radically different from those presented above. They believed that it was not true that the Slavs appeared in Poland only in the 5th and 6th centuries, but they were the eternal inhabitants of these lands. It is impossible to investigate these matters in relation to even earlier times, but the Lusatian culture, so-called archaeologists, one of the greatest archaeological cultures of the barbarian Europe of the Bronze Age and the Early Iron Age, which developed in areas from central

Elbe in the west to the south-east Polish. Lusatian culture was certainly already created by the Slavs. This means that the Slavs have been hosts on the central Elbe, Oder and Vistula since at least around 1300 BC, and maybe longer. Lusatian culture was not created from a vacuum, but had to take shape against some background, grow out of some earlier cultures. The argument that the Roman authors, when writing about Polish lands, mention only Germanic tribes, consists either of a misunderstanding, because the Romans did not know these areas very well and generally were dependent on the accounts of their mostly German informants or on erroneous scientific interpretation. Perhaps, finally, the accounts of the Romans could also be basically accurate, nevertheless, the stay of peoples or rather smaller groups of the Germanic population in the Polish lands was now irrelevant and episodic, and in the

Roman period the only significant ethnic element on the Oder and Vistula was Slavic peoples.

Cultural continuity?

The question arises how "neoautochthonists" determined the ethnic face of the Sorbian culture? Perhaps they did it, according to their own judgment, as follows. They probably came from the state of material and spiritual culture of the Slavs from the 6th and 7th centuries, because there is no doubt as to the Slavic origin of the archaeological material of the Polish lands of that time, they went back, reaching in turn the older, preceding the Slavonic archeological cultures. Archaeologists have thus found fundamental developmental continuity. So they used the so-called retrogression method, i.e. the transition from better known later facts to less well recognized events from earlier times. Thus archaeologists received approximately the following sequence of cultures:

"early Slavic" culture since the 6th century,

cultures of the Roman period, i.e. the culture of cavity graves,
which includes two cultures: Przeworsk and Oksyiv,
from the end of the 2nd century BC until the turn of the 4th and 5th centuries CE or even slightly longerPomeranian culture,
 otherwise known as East Pomerania, the culture of box graves, the culture of face urns,
 and recently even the Wejherowo-Krotoszyn culture) and its partially contemporary culture of subclave graves,
 both were considered derivatives of the Sorbian culture.

The alleged continuity of cultures was confirmed on the basis of various arguments: the main convergence of classes and lifestyles of the Lusatian culture tribes and Slavs in the early Middle Ages was emphasized, among others forms of tools or households, and the emerging differences were considered accidental and irrelevant. It was argued that since in the Polish lands since the middle phase of the Bronze Age, i.e. around 1300 B.C.E. until the early Middle Ages you can see a clear sequence of archaeological cultures, apparently all this time the land was inhabited by the same Slavic population.

Currently, neither one of the views outlined here convinces archaeologists. There is insufficient evidence to recognize the Sorbian culture as Germanic. Even German scholars quickly abandoned this view, because there are serious reasons against the mechanical connection of the Lusatian culture with the Slavs. Attention is drawn to the irregularity of the research procedure of "neo-autochthonists" who accept elements of culture that testify to the continuity of this culture, and to omit or disregard elements that could rather prove otherwise, as well as inappropriate and methodological premises imposed by the other party, among others identifying archaeological cultures with ethnos. Currently, weak spots are also noticed in the reconstructed arduously string of cultures allegedly derived from each other. So far, two major gaps in this chain have not been filled. One of them covers the fifth century AD, which on the archaeological map of Poland is still marked with a white spot, and the other relates to the 3rd and 2nd centuries BC, which is the middle phase of the Late period, when the Lusatian, Pomeranian and sub-fossil graves have passed away, but they did not manage to form. still culture of cavity graves: Przeworsk and Oksywska.

In this way a problem arose and actually continues to this day, because since the Lusatian culture can no longer be attributed to either Germans or Slavs, scholars (German scholars excel in it) came up with the idea of attributing it to the lyre of the well-witnessed and known ancient people living in the western part Balkans. According to archaeologists, this would be completely unknown until now, and according to many scholars, being a mere scientific fiction, the northern branch of this people. Some scholars were in favor of polyethnicity, i.e. multi-ethnicity of the Sorbian culture. According to this theory, the western part of the Lusatian culture would be the work of some other Illyrians or Venedians, which I will write below, while the eastern Zawisian work of the Slavs, because the Eastern Tertiary culture is the oldest archaeological equivalent of the Slavs. There was also a view among researchers that the feature of the earliest distinguishing feature of the Slavic population should be attributed to the culture of sub-flared graves from the late Bronze Age and the early Iron Age. Archaeologists, faced with the problem of the impossibility or difficulty in connecting Lusatian culture with specific Indo-European peoples of Europe, came to the conviction of the exclusive, or at least to a large extent, its creation by some people who no longer existed. The thoughts of archaeologists focus on the one hand on the Old Europeans already mentioned to us in linguistic analyzes, and on the other towards the mysterious Venetians mentioned in ancient sources. Therefore, at this point in the work, we will devote some time to the accounts of ancient writers.

Relations of ancient authors

What did ancient writers know about Polish lands? Source studies show that really little. The Greeks knew the northern Black Sea coast inhabited by Scythian peoples relatively accurately. Herodotus of Halicarnassus in the 5th century BC he mentioned the people of Nurów, which he probably located in the south-eastern borderlands of the former Polish-Lithuanian Commonwealth, perhaps in Podolia and Volhynia, which gave some scholars an impulse to connect this name with the Slavs. They pointed out, among others on the core nur-, ner-, found in some river names in Slavic. This is only a separate hypothesis that is difficult to analyze historically. There was also the view that Nurów Herodot can be identified with one of the local high groups of the Lusatian culture, but the possibility is not subject to scientific verification.

A few centuries later, when the primacy in the ancient world shifted from ancient Greece to ancient Rome, they appeared in the ancient literature more concretely and already analyzing information about the Polish lands and the peoples inhabiting them. In ancient Rome, it was known about the Baltic Sea and the Gulf of Gdansk, they occurred, for example, in Ptolemy under the names of the Sarmatian Ocean and the Gulf of Venedia, about the mountains of the Venedic Mountains, the Carpathian Mountains, Askiburgion - probably a mountain range in the Sudetes, Vistula was known under the names Vistla, Vistula, much weaker Odra under a different name, of the "cities" located in the territories of later Poland by Ptolemy, only the famous Kalisia pretends in a sense to identify with Kalisz on Prosna, although this is argued by historians.

Sources, mainly Tacitus and Ptolemy, enumerate many peoples living in Polish or neighboring lands. Their names are ethnically foreign (Germanic, Celtic, Thracian) or belong to the Baltic peoples who have undeniable historical rights to their lands in the south-eastern region of the Baltic Sea, but in part they cannot be identified with any known historians. The most important from the point of view of the Slavic ethnogenesis are the names of Lugrów and Wenedów (Wenedów).

Lugii

Indisputable sources from antiquity, works of Strabon, Tacitus, and Ptolemy confirm the existence in the first centuries of our era, most likely in the southwestern part of Polish lands, a tribe or several tribes called Lugiowie. Tacitus states that to the north of the mountains (probably the Sudetes) the name Lugia sounds the loudest. Ptolemy lists their three factions, while the oldest of the three writers Strabon confirms the difference between the Lugras and the undoubtedly Germanic Siewów. Who were the Lugi who later completely disappear from the source? Some regarded them as Germanic, others as Slavs, because in their tribal name the Slavic lug-, łęg-, who were seen, who would leave the Sorbs. Still others may have rightly considered them to be Celts, who, however, a little earlier, because in the last three centuries BC they mastered certain areas of Silesia and western

Lesser Poland. However, the Celts could hardly disappear overnight, although looking at it in terms of the Przeworsk culture of the Roman period it is replacing one unknown with another. They were created as a tribal union, which was established to control the famous Amber Route, connecting the amber-producing coast of the Baltic Sea, primarily Sambia, with the northern coast of the Adriatic Sea, and with it the entire Roman world. It is not clear, however, what this function of Lugia would consist of and how to reconcile the contradictions with the assumption that in their case it could be a polyethylene creation, a conglomerate of multilingual tribes, with the participation of Celts, Germanes (since some of the Lugian tribes have clearly Germanic names) and Slavs.

Weneds

Pliny the Elder in the first century C.E. noted the name Wenedów among other peoples. The context of this part of Natural History shows that they inhabited approximately the area of Polish Pomerania. The people of the same name mention, and also bluntly characterize Tacitus later, saying that they occupy huge areas between the Fennas, Finno-Ugric peoples of north-eastern Europe, and the Bastards, also quite a mysterious Celtic or Germanic people, specifically the faction of the people that under the name At that time Peukin lived near the mouth of the Danube. Unfortunately, Tacitus wrote about the Wenedów headquarters in very general terms, but historians say that this description indicates areas located east of the Vistula River and the Carpathian Arch.

In the consciousness of Tacitus, and his ancient erudites today, the belief that the whole, little-known to the Greeks and Romans of the northern part of the world, can be attributed to the Germans, with whom the Romans came into contact on the Rhine and the Danube, and the Sarmatians who at that time drove the Scythians from the steppes over In a way the Black Sea and in the consciousness of the ancients they somewhat replaced them as barbarians. Tacitus could not imagine that between the Germans and the nomadic Sarmatians there could be some other tribes, e.g. Slavic. Probably the great personality of Tacitus, like his contemporaries, operated on a completely different understanding of the terms "Germans" and "Sarmatians". For us, these are ethnic concepts and mean peoples speaking Germanic or Iranian Indo-European languages.

Tacitus probably had no idea what languages these barbarians speak, but he pointed out the essential features of their existence and culture. He understood the "Sarmatians" as nomadic peoples, and at this point the cultural concept coincided with the ethnic one; and with the term "Germananie" the situation got complicated, resulting in a lot of confusion in science.

Since, in the most famous last, forty-sixth chapter of his treatise, Germania Tacitus hesitated whether he should classify the Venedians, Bastarns, and Fenes to the Germans or to the Sarmatians, the above conclusion seems to be fully justified.

Tacitus wrote:

The Weneds took a lot from the customs of the Sarmatians, because in their plundering expeditions all forests and mountains that rise between the Peukins and Fennas run. Rather, however, they should be among the Germans. Because they build permanent houses, wear shields, enjoy walking and walking - all this is different for Sarmatians who spend their lives on a cart and horse.

Certainly, based on the accounts of Tacitus, one should not extend the seats of Germanic tribes to Eastern Europe and consider Venetians as Germanic in the current ethnic meaning of the word, although historians have often put forward theses that were difficult to prove.

Ptolemy's "Sarmation"

Unlike the historian Tacitus, the geographer Ptolemy gives more data that makes it easier to place on the map of Venets. This Alexandrian erudite divided today's Polish lands into two parts separated by the Vistula and allocated them to larger geographical and ethnic units. He connected the part located west of the Vistula to "Great Germania" (germania megale), while the part located east - to European Sarmatia. Great Germania stretched from the Rhine to the Vistula, European Sarmatia - from the Vistula to Don (Tanais); further between Don and Volga was the second Sarmatia - Asian, but she is not interested in us at the moment. In Germany, in its eastern "Polish" part he mentioned, among others three of them from the aforementioned Lugia and the city of Kalisia. However, according to him, there are a lot of tribes with different names in Sarmatia, whose recognition or even identification has already been a dream to many historians.

At this point I would like to deal with only one, but for us the most important people of Ptolemy's European Sarmatation - Wenedami.

Ptolemy, after presenting the location of this Sarmatia, wrote:

Huge peoples live in Sarmatia: the Venedians along the entire Venedic Gulf, above the Dacia Peukins and Basterns (...)

For the sake of clarity, I will not mention further "huge peoples" of Sarmatia, because they do not connect directly with our topic of reflection.

The quotation above shows that Ptolemy's Wenedes occupy a place analogous to the Tacitus Wenedes in his geographical and ethnic system, which means that they were the main ethnic factor of Eastern Europe east of the Vistula, not counting Bastards, Iranian-speaking peoples.

In the next sentence of his work Ptolemy began to enumerate the lesser peoples of European Sarmatia. He started from the western, i.e. from the Vistula ranks, and went from the north, that is from the Baltic Sea, from the Gulf of Wenedia to the south. The beginning of this series of peoples is as follows:

Of the smaller peoples, Gytonowie sit in Sarmatia near the Wistula River, below the Wenedów; then Finns, then Sulons; below them the Frugundions, then the Avarins near the sources of the Wistula River.

[And] more to the east than those mentioned here Ptolemy proceeded to enumerate the second meridional sequence of "Sarmatian" peoples sitting beneath the Venedes Galindowie, Sudinów and Stawanów up to Alanów, etc.

Perhaps the word below in Ptolemy probably means south, from the last quote quoted it would appear that the southern, or more precisely the south-eastern neighbors of the Wenedes were Galinds. This information is quite troublesome, because the Galinds, as well as the next Sudinians in the list, belong to this category of names in Ptolemy, which can be identified and localized relatively confidently. The Galinds and Sudins belong to the Baltic tribes, they are more precisely known only from the Middle Ages, but the Balts in science are attributed, not without reason, the exceptional stability of their seats, which were almost certainly in the area of today's Masuria. If, indeed, this was the case in Ptolemy's day, the Wenedes, who named the bay and the mountains, just characterized by the same author as a powerful people and probably a really great people, they would turn out to be not very impressive people occupying modest headquarters east of the Vistula, right on the sea.

Such a conclusion would find additional confirmation in the previous quote. If the Galinds were adjacent to the Wenedes from the south-east, then the Gytons were supposed to be living directly south of the latter. Under this name, many scholars see Germanic, well-known Goths in later times. It is known about these people that around the turn of the old and new era he moved from Scandinavia and began his journey south, which for some time also stopped them in the territory of northern Poland. Anyway, in accordance with the later Gothic tradition, recorded by Goth by origin, historian Jordanes, the Goths' continental seats were sought rather in Gdańsk Pomerania. Meanwhile, Ptolemy places Python as if at some distance from the sea below the Venedes. In the latest science, there was a belief, based on the analysis of archaeological material, that these seats were probably located somewhat inland on the Vistula, more or less in the region of Toruń. This would exactly match Ptolemy's data if, which is not certain, the thesis of German archaeologist Rolf Hachmann was to remain in science.

Not the Goths will interest me right now, but the Weneds. The contradiction of information about this people in Ptolemy's work is obvious. The Weneds could not be a great people reaching south only to the headquarters of the Vistula Goths, Galinds and Sudans. Could Ptolemy be wrong? Some scholars believe that only the first mention of Ptolemy of the great people refers to the real Wenedes, while the small people of the Wenedes make a mistake, which is possible, since such errors did not occur in the Alexandrian erudite. Perhaps the Venedes in the latter sense appear in his work instead of the Aists, an ancient Prussian people known long before Ptolemy, whose seats would in fact correspond to the data of our author about the small Wenedas? It is difficult to say why Ptolemy does not mention the Aistas. Of course, the easiest solution would be to accuse the old author of a mistake when his information does not agree with our perceptions of the past and try to improve it. However, in this case such an amendment seems relatively well justified, although I am in favor of it in the form of a cautious hypothesis.

Thanks to it, Tacitus and Ptolemy's data on Wenedas were harmonized. In summary, the Weneds were at the beginning of our era a significant people living in large, impossible to define areas east of the Vistula. It seems reasonable to suppose that the Wenedes were then the main ethnic factor in these areas, hence our interest in them.

Wenedowie / Weds - "Praslavs"?

Two questions arise that I would like to answer later in this work. Who were the Wenedes? Can they be identified with any other European people we know?

In Polish science, the belief that the ancient Venets were identical with the Proslovans became widespread. This is also due to the assumption that the Praslavs had inhabited Polish lands for many centuries before Ptolemy, as well as from other source data. The most important argument for the thesis is that later, Byzantine and Latin writers, starting from Jordanes in the mid-sixth century very often used the term Wenedowie or Venetians (these two terms are equivalent) to describe the Slavs. In addition, the Germans still in the Middle Ages and later called the Slavs Wenedami (die Wenden). Meanwhile, the Finns reportedly still speak about the Eastern Slavs they only knew, Venaja. "If we consider the Venedians as Praslavs, we identify them with the creators of the archaeological culture of cavity tombs (i.e. the same name derives from the Senedi language. Meanwhile, it is completely impossible, since the name sounds Venetian correctly, and the Venedi is a Germanic form. where the Slavs certainly were not. The name Venetians derives from the element mend-, which means a loving family, belonging to the family, a relative. The most famous example of this name is the name of the famous Venice on the Adriatic, but the Venets, first mentioned by Homer in Iliad as Enetoi in the territory of Paflagonia in Asia Minor, occupied headquarters from Wales and Brittany in the west clothing to the Balkan peninsula and Little Asia in the east.

How can this phenomenon be explained? Is the accidental equivalence of the names of peoples having nothing in common? This is rather unbelievable. Or perhaps the spatial dispersion of "Venetian" names documents a huge area once inhabited a long time ago by one great Venetian people; and the Venetians, Welsh, Welsh, Gallic, Vistula, Adriatic, Lesser-Asian etc. would only be the remains of this great people? There may be another possibility. the presence of Venetian names throughout almost all of Europe is perhaps the result of the expansion of Venets, taken from one more restricted region.

The second option presented inevitably leads to the identification of Venets with Old Europeans, whose existence we know only thanks to the inquiries of linguists. The Venetian nomenclature, however, goes beyond the area of the Old European language established by linguists, in addition, we know, although only partially, the language of the Adriatic Venetians, only people have more historical knowledge about this, which is not surprising due to the vicinity of Rome. It turns out that it was not identical to the reconstructed Old European language, but it was a separate, developed Indo-European language, closely related to Illyrian and Italian. We cannot reproduce the language of the Breton Venetian, Vistula, etc., even to the extent that, but by adopting the genetic link between individual Venetian branches, we tend to favor the third of the outlined possibilities. However, it is difficult to agree on science in this complex issue, and scientists tried to locate the original Venetian headquarters in various places in Europe. I propose to adopt the recently formulated, following the assumptions of the German linguist Paul Kretschmer, the thesis of Gerard Labuda. According to it, the seats of the Venets in the Bronze Age were between the middle Elbe and the lower Vistula, mainly in the Odra basin. Venets neighbors there first with the Celts, Lyres and Italics, and then also with the Germans, Balts and Praslovans. The Lusatian culture was the archaeological equivalent of the Venets. Around 1000 BC Venetian migrations began up to about the middle of the first millennium before Christ. They caused, on the one hand, the spread of Venetian names in large areas of Europe, and on the other, a significant thinning and weakening of Venetian settlement in the native area. Archaeological process marked by the decay and decline of the Sorbian culture.

The Vistula Venetian area was penetrated by other peoples: Scythian invasions from the east, Celtic pressure from the south, Germans from the north, and above all the Venetian headquarters in the eastern part of the Venetian territory were occupied gradually and permanently by Praslavs. In this way, the Prussians entered as if they had occupied the areas previously occupied by the Venets, we have no reason to believe that this was happening in a mild manner and, as a consequence, the name Venetians was transferred to the Slavs probably by Germanic neighbors.

Certainly in the 6th century it already meant Slavs. It is difficult to say now whether in the first and second centuries, that is when the names Wenedowie were used by Pliny, Tacitus and Ptolemy were they Slavs? We are not sure about this, although it is not excluded. This does not mean at all that on the lower Vistula and east of this river in Roman times there was a close-knit Olden ethnic group that had not yet undergone Balticisation or Slavization. During the reign of Emperor Nero a certain agile Roman went in search of amber to the Baltic. It is not excluded that Gerard Labuda admits that this first tourist known from sources in Poland communicated with the local population through the accompanying Venets from the Po River. However, considering all the pros and cons, I am inclined, however, to agree more likely with the "Slavic" thesis.

The Venetians of Pliny, and probably Tacitus and Ptolemy, mean Proslavs. With this assumption, it is not true that ancient sources do not know the Slavs, that the Slavs are the "great absentee" of European history at that time.

A new approach to the ethnogenesis of the Slavs

Until recently, the above argument would not have met with major opposition in Polish science. A few years ago, however, Krakow's pre-historian Kazimierz Godłowski thoroughly criticized this approach and proposed a completely different from his predecessors, typically allochtonistic solution to the problem of the ethnogenesis of the Slavs.

According to Kazimierz Godłowski, ancient and early Byzantine sources were not wrong about the Slavs, giving them under different names. According to him, the Slavs as a separate ethnic entity did not exist before the fifth and sixth centuries AD. Early Slavic culture, which from the sixth century, in some areas maybe even from the late fifth century; it was extremely difficult to undergo closer chronological treatment. It appeared in vast areas of Eastern, Central and Southeastern Europe from the central Dnieper and Pripyat basins in the east to the Elbe, Sala and Men in the west and almost the entire Balkan Peninsula. In its initial phase it was extremely compact throughout its territory, and at the same time completely different from the cultures preceding it in the area north of the mountains of Central and Eastern Europe - Sudety, Carpathians. I am talking here about the Przeworsk and oxywska cultures in the Odra and Vistula basins and the so-called Zarubiniec culture (named after the city of Zarubincy) on the central Dnieper, developing from about the 2nd century BC until II CE century. For supporters of the "macro-homeland" of the Slavs, among others for P. N. Tertiaków, these cultures were simply equivalent to the Western Slavs, as well as to the Przeworsk and oxyiv cultures, as well as the Eastern (Zarubuniec) cultures. According to Kazimierz Godłowski, this cannot be said. All the similarities observed in science between the early Slavic culture from the 6th and 8th centuries, and the above-mentioned cultures of the Roman period are of secondary nature, significant and significant are the differences.

These differences are:

developed, specialized craftsmanship, primarily within the Przeworsk culture; pottery workshops worked too; iron metallurgy, which in the huge Świętokrzyskie Basin, where there is now an archaeological reserve, has achieved admirable momentum and had to supply much of Europe, some scholars claim that even the Roman Empire; this culture was different from the primitive, non-specialized, working only for their own use crafts of the Slavs of the 6th-8th century,knowledge of a potter's wheel, diversity and high technological level of pottery in the Roman period, and primitive, undifferentiated, molded exclusively by hand from brown clay with a large admixture of sand, "early Slavic" ceramics, mainly high pots of the "Prague" or "Korczak" type (from the city of Korczak near Żytomierz), occurring in a few varieties in large areas occupied by the Slavs in the early Middle Ages, only in the area of Ukraine was accompanied by the Slavs slightly more developed "Pieńkowka" ceramics,rich equipment of graves in the Roman period and extremely poverty of "early Slavic" graves, where ashtrails (ashtrays usually represent Prague type ceramics) contain almost no items accompanying the deceased. One may think that this is about deliberate ritual poverty, caused by cultural reasons (it is about not placing weapons, tools, decorations in graves), were it not for the fact that also Slavic settlement finds unearthed by archaeologists are with very few exceptions. These observations confirmed the belief in the low level of development of crafts, especially metallurgical Slavs in the sixth and subsequent centuries.

The settlements of the sixth and seventh centuries themselves were initially small open settlements, most often located on rivers, on river terraces or in the valleys themselves. They often form small clusters. Large areas of early medieval Slavs were characterized by small houses, most often square half-dunes, with a stove or hearth in the corner.

We will not discuss the ceramics patterns, a problem that does not apply here, by referring the reader to the following list of references.

Very compact and covering almost the entire area in which in the early Middle Ages written sources attested to the presence of the Slavs, the set of cultural features discussed is characterized by:

Not so much a specific set of guiding types of movable monuments as the general model and structure of this culture, reflecting a specific type of economic and social relations, settlement, customs and beliefs [Kazimierz Godłowski].

Kazimierz Godłowski came to the conclusion that the described cultural model was first created in Ukraine between the Eastern Carpathians and the Dnieper. There, from the end of the 4th century, the disappearance of earlier cultures - the Chernihiv and so-called Carpathian burial mounds, there or in the eastern part of the Vistula river basin

(...) crystallization of this culture took place in the fifth century and here was also the starting area for its further expansion.

This crystallization, named by Kazimierz Godłowski, means that only from that moment on, i.e. from the fifth to the sixth century, one can talk about Slavs and their culture at all. This culture cannot be derived from any other culture and it is an innovation. However, archaeological observations seem to indicate that the decisive share in the formation of Slavic culture in the V and VI centuries was the population from areas located north of the forest zone of Eastern Europe. Around 520, the second stage of Slavic expansion begins, which brought the Slavs huge gains and about 20% of the continent's area.

It can be seen that Kazimierz Godłowski changed the approach of historians and archaeologists to the topic of Slavic ethnogenesis. He also ended the researchers' dispute on this fascinating topic. He believed that searching for Slavs in the Roman period and even in the earlier period was a futile occupation, because the Slavs did not yet exist at that time. In addition, in modern science, not only Kazimierz Godłowski came to the conclusion that the process of crystallization of the Slavic ethos came so late. A similar view was also recently formulated by the Czech scholar Zdenek Van. The founding of Kazmierz Godłowski met with varied reception in Polish science. Supporters of traditional views and the so-called "long genealogy" of the Slavs. Quite obviously, they took a negative view of Godłowski's thesis.

However, according to Gerard Labuda, it does not explain all doubts. There is a contradiction in the results of the linguistics and prehistory studies. For example, linguists state that the most archaic Slavic names appear above the upper Prut, the Dniester and Bohem, and partly also in the upper Vistula basin. Meanwhile, Godłowski excludes that the Pruty and Dniester basin was inhabited by the Slavs during the Roman influence. The second argument of linguists is that all the basic names of rivers in Poland that are suspected of Venetian origin, that is, those taken over by the Slavs directly from the Venetian language, cannot be taken directly from Venetians without the German intermediation. The question arises to what extent is this linguistic thesis correct? The Slavs would have to live in Poland much earlier than in the fifth and sixth centuries CE, when significant groups of the Old Venetian population were still here.

PART I

To be continued

Lawrence Querengesser

Printed in Great Britain
by Amazon

16943709R00058